Simple Decorative Paper Techniques

Stéphane Ipert and
Florent Rousseau

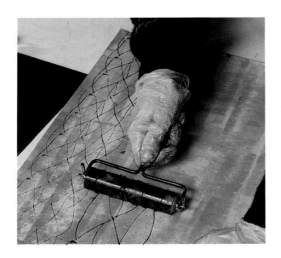

SEARCH PRESS

First published in Great Britain 1992
Search Press Limited,
Wellwood, North Farm Road,
Tunbridge Wells, Kent TN2 3DR

English translation copyright © Search Press
Limited 1992

Originally published in France
by Dessain et Tolra, Paris

Copyright © Dessain et Tolra 1988

Translated by Giles de la Bedoyère

We wish to thank in particular the following:
Mrs J. Rousseau, Mrs G. Noel and Mrs S.
Evrard, for their help and support. Gratitude is
also due to the Studio of Applied Arts of Vésinet
who lent us their space and materials.

ISBN 0 85532 728 6

There are references to the use of solvents
in this book. These substances should be
handled with care.

- All solvents should be kept in sealed
  containers out of the reach of children.
- Solvents are poisonous.
  Do not inhale vapours.
- Solvents are highly inflammable.
  Do not smoke when using them.
- Work in a well-aired room and wear
  plastic gloves.

Composition by Genesis Typesetting,
Laser Quay, Rochester, Kent
Printed in Singapore by Huntsmen Offset Printing Pte Ltd

Contents

Introduction

The blank sheet of paper which may terrify the would-be author can also provide the means of creating a fantasy. Whether the original paper is simply painted in a single colour, printed with an all-over pattern or painted with a medium to which paste has been added, this craft offers a wide variety of designs and a diversity of different methods.

No specific artistic knowledge is required and this book concentrates on techniques rather than artistic originality. In fact, it can be argued that the skill of the artisan is the basis of all art.

The initial outlay for materials and equipment is very modest and only amounts to sheets of suitable plain paper, jars of paint or ink in various colours, sponges, brushes and a paint roller. Step-by-step instructions will show you how to create stippled and stencilled

patterns, or abstract designs using inked rollers, resist techniques and a method of batik.

Paper decorated in this way has many uses, ranging from book covers to your own highly original wrapping-paper for personal gifts, or even as a pictorial composition in its own right. As you continue to experiment with the ideas featured in this book, you will find more ways of expressing your own creativity with this unusual and exciting craft.

History

The story of paper decoration obviously relates to that of the history of paper itself. This was a Chinese invention dating from the beginning of our era, believed to be by Ts'ai Lun in AD105.

Used first as a functional writing surface, paper gradually acquired colouring, each tint having a particular significance. Yellow, for instance, contained a preservative which repelled insects. Simple colouring then gave way to greater sophistication of technique, in line with Chinese aesthetic taste and an example of this would be the famous 'Albums of Ten Bamboos'. Later still, gold and silver enriched paper designs appeared, then, about the tenth century, painting with a medium to which paste had been added, and striped or spotted papers became fashionable.

Around the eighth century, the Japanese acquired knowledge of the Chinese techniques of papermaking, and rapidly imposed their own artistic variations. Paper decoration in Japan took on a cultural and traditional importance and reached a high level of quality and craftsmanship, which gave rise to folded and tinted papers, 'batik' papers, and papers printed by 'masking'. Coloured silk fibres were also incorporated into the actual manufacture of the paper.

The Islamic world inherited this developed industry after the battle of Tallas, near Samarkand, in the ninth century, and it flourished under the Ottoman and Moghul dynasties. Designs were abstract, since this religion forbids figurative representation and the sacred texts were subtly integrated with the decorations, which enhanced each page as well as the binding of each manuscript.

Techniques continued to be explored and even more exciting methods came into use. Colours were sprayed on to plain or masked papers, or impregnated to give a grained effect.

6

Plate showing various crafts. Embossed and gilded relief on a green background. The Hague.

It was only in the fifteenth and sixteenth centuries that this Oriental art appeared in Europe, in the form of impressionist effects on painted wallpapers. Painting with added paste became popular in France, Italy and Germany in many designer-equipped studios or workshops. The seventeenth and eighteenth centuries, however, witnessed a full flowering of paper decoration, as bookbindings, book endpapers and covers, and for using shell motifs, pebbling, spattering and combed effects. In Germany, papers were printed and embossed with copper and silver leaf over a background of plain, or tinted painting on paste.

Opposite: **Miniature painted in indian ink, showing a hunting scene.**
National Museum of New Delhi.

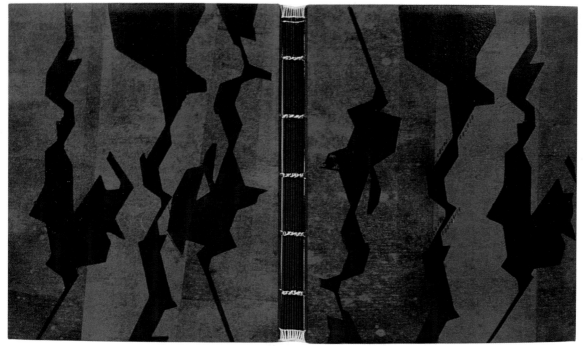

Bookbinding. Covers decorated with direct printing over a uniform background of soluble ink. *Florent Rousseau.*

Mechanization dominated everything, including the production of decorated papers in the early nineteenth century, and this led to an increasing excess and abuse of design. In Britain, the poet and craftsman, William Morris, was to have an enormous effect on the style of the period and he gathered many like-minded artists and craftsmen around him. His dislike of the earlier ugliness of the century and his belief that beauty and equality should be available to all mankind did much to improve the standard of ordinary domestic decorations, such as wallpapers, fabrics and tiles. From his teachings came the belief that the artisan was as important as the artist.

The twentieth century has seen ever-increasing technical advances and we have lost many of our previous manual skills. In spite of, or maybe because of it, more and more people are turning to arts and crafts which will enable them to express their own creativity.

Papers and pigments

Papers

Choice of paper is an important determining factor in the type of decoration to be applied, and certain materials are suited only to particular surfaces. Imagine the difference between working on blotting-paper, tracing-paper, cloth-based paper and gloss-coated paper! For each type of paper, there is a specific method of application and knowledge of their individual composition is helpful.

Paper is composed of various vegetable fibres, from rag and from wood-pulp, or a mixture of these materials. Rag paper is usually of better quality than the wood-based variety.

The following information about some of the different types of paper which are available, will enable you to choose the best material for your purpose.

Identification of paper

Certain papers are imprinted in their manufacture and if held up to the light, reveal closely set perpendicular markings or 'watermarks'.

These are called 'wired' or 'laid' papers, from the French word 'verge', for example, *Ingres* papers. These watermarks may indicate logos and brand names of the manufacturers, but the best known use of this method is in banknotes.

Plain, unmarked paper is called 'vellum', and this is suitable for most methods of decoration.

Single grain paper

The way of laying the fibres in some papers produces 'graining' in a single direction and, if wetted, it will expand in that direction, rather than the opposite way. 'Wired' or 'laid' paper grain follows the direction of the watermarks.

Other types of paper must be tested by wetting a sample. First wet the paper with a brush, or rub sufficient water on with thumb and index finger along the borders, then observe which sides elongate. For some kinds of paper used for covering books and as packaging, it is essential to follow the grain in order to avoid bending or tension problems.

Weight of paper

All papers have a certain weight per square metre (yard). For example, writing paper is usually between 80–100gm (3–4oz) but watercolour paper may be as much as 300gm (12oz).

Texture of surface

This varies from smooth, hot-pressed paper, to rough handmade rag paper.

Power of absorption

Writing paper is gummed so as not to absorb ink but blotting-paper is not. Gloss-coated paper only absorbs certain inks.

Strength

This depends upon the thickness of the paper, the quality of the gumming, and the length of fibres in its composition. Some papers are very fragile and will require special precautions when handling.

Single-ply paper

This is almost transparent and is extremely difficult to handle. Special Japanese silk papers give the best effects.

Colours

The choice of inks and paints will depend upon the type of paper to be used and the method of application to be employed.

Suitable materials may be obtained in art and craft shops, and they can be purchased in tubes or jars. It is necessary to experiment with varied brands to determine their suitability for your purpose. Some only work best for particular techniques, while others adapt well to any form of decorating on paper.

Oil and acrylic paints and various inks are all useful. The latter may be in liquid form, such as indian ink, or solid, oil-based printing ink. Colour changes depend upon the reaction of the eyes of each individual to light, but they divide into three main groups; primary colours, secondary colours and tertiary colours.

Primary colours

Blue, red and yellow are the three basic colours and these can be mixed to obtain almost any hue.

Secondary colours

Orange, purple and green, are derived from the mixture of any two primaries, e.g. green, from blue and yellow. Together, primary and secondary groups form the spectrum of the rainbow.

Tertiary colours

These are obtained by mixing primaries with secondaries, and produce yellow-green, blue-green, blue-violet, yellow-orange, red-violet and red-orange.

Identifying colours

Red, yellow, orange and their derivatives are called 'warm' colours, whereas blue, green and violet are called 'cold'. The degrees of warmth and cold are relative, however, as a lemon yellow, for instance, approaches the cold palette by its tendency towards green, a cold hue.

The 'tone' of a colour indicates its degree of darkness or lightness, e.g. dark blue, light blue, and so on.

Colour intensity indicates its degree of brilliance. An admixture of grey will reduce this, according to the amount used. The primary colours in order of their intensity, are red, the highest, yellow and then blue, the lowest.

Plain and tinted surfaces

Elementary techniques will soon enable you to become familiar with different types of paper, as well as tools and materials. They show how to obtain plain or varied backgrounds, which may be left as complete or serve as a basis for imposed decoration at a later stage.

Spotted effect. *Stéphane Ipert.*

Plain papers

Requirements

A resistant, non-absorbent paper must be used. You will also need jars for mixing the paints, sponges, brushes and a roller. Every method requires its special pigments, either pure or diluted.

Acrylic colours for plain papers

Acrylic colours sold in tubes, are easy to use and are very brilliant.

Application Acrylic colours are applied with a sponge roller whose breadth must be at least 15cm (6in). Add a little water to expediate the flow. Saturate the roller evenly, then cover the sheet of paper with a regular application, using strokes which cross each other to ensure a uniform finish.

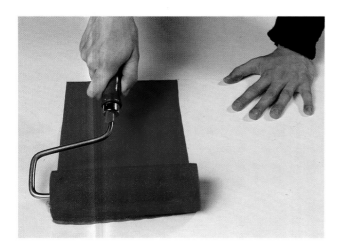

Aerosol cans of acrylic may also be used, as long as the manufacturer's instructions are followed. Keep the nozzle at the prescribed distance from the paper and avoid dwelling on one spot, to make sure it is not overloaded with pigment. After application, leave the paper lying flat to dry for several hours.

Soluble ink for plain pastel papers

For this type of effect, you must use special soluble inks, notable for their luminosity.

Application Dampen the paper with a sponge. Saturate another sponge with colour, squeeze it out, and then apply it regularly to the sheet of paper from top to bottom. You must work quickly to obtain a unified effect, without overlaying the colour-washes.

Leave the sheet of paper, lying flat, to dry and then use a special fixative applied with a spray can over the whole area.

Oil-based printing ink for plain pastel papers

Dilute the colours with white spirit. A walnut-sized amount of pigment to a jar of the dilution is sufficient. In order to test the permanency of the colour after drying, test a sample of your mixture on similar paper beforehand.

Application This is as given for soluble inks, but these colours do not require fixing.

13

Multicoloured papers

These provide a suitable basis for other methods of decoration, which can later be applied to the background. Use soluble colours, such as indian or soluble ink, and a semi-absorbent paper, such as watercolour paper, or a loose weave paper.

Preparation of colours

Pure pigments produce strong tonal contrasts of colour, so it is advisable to dilute them if a softer, pastel effect is required.

Pour your colours, diluted or not, into glass jars, and prepare a sponge dipped in the first colour to be used.

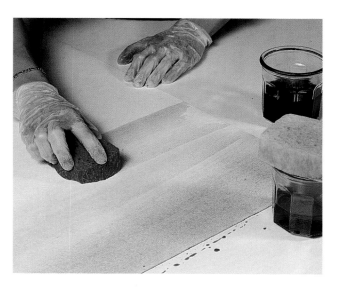

Application

Lightly dampen your sheet of paper, then with the sponge in the first colour to be used, squeeze out the colour gently, and apply it from top to bottom of the paper. Begin again with a second sponge and apply your second tint, overlapping the first application to obtain the gradation. Avoid going over the same place twice, so that the result has a regular effect, otherwise the whole process may have to be repeated! Leave the sheet flat to dry, then fix as given on page 13.

Example of a gradated wash. Florent Rousseau.

'Spot and sprinkle' effects

These are variations of the previous technique, obtained by a haphazard application of pigments, whether with cotton wool or an eye-dropper.

Equipment and materials

Identical paper and colours as given for the multicoloured background, some rolls of cotton wool and an eye-dropper.

Application

Dampen the paper with a sponge. Pour a little colour on to one of the dampened rolls of cotton wool, then apply this with a circular motion to the paper. Do this all over, occasionally renewing the colour on your cotton wool, thus obtaining a basic background. Then, fill the eye-dropper with a new colour and sprinkle a few drops over the whole area, according to your own taste. Repeat with a third and fourth colour varying your design. Leave to dry, then fix as given on page 13.

'Spot' effect over a unified background, which has been retouched with a soft brush. *Florent Rousseau.*

Variation

A gilded effect can now be added to the background. You will require some powdered gold paint from an art shop, plus an alcohol, such as lighter fuel.

Pour about half a teaspoonful of gold on to a sheet of paper, then holding this above the painted paper, blow the powder on to your design as evenly as possible. Don't overdo the gold. Fill the eye-dropper with the alcohol and apply regularly spaced drops over the surface about every 2cm (¾ in). The alcohol causes the gold to draw together into irregular spots. Leave to dry, then fix.

'Spot' effect. The colour is applied with an eye-dropper over a damp surface.

Spattering

It is best to use indian or Chinese inks because of their greater brilliance. They should be used pure and undiluted.

You will also require a small metallic grille, such as a strainer, and a stiff brush which will ensure an even and effective distribution of colour.

Application

Before beginning, try out your technique on newspaper, so as to remove some of the surplus colour. Then carefully spread the pigment over your sheet of paper by rubbing your brush over the grille, applying it continuously from left to right, or from top to bottom so that the spattering is evenly distributed. Remember to wash out both brush and grille before embarking on any fresh colour.

You can obtain a delightful multicoloured effect, by positioning masks of different shapes, round, rectangular, square etc., on the paper to block out certain areas. These should be cut from stiff paper or cardboard. With each rearrangement of these masks, apply a new colour. The superimposition of painted areas will achieve interesting and artistic designs. Leave to dry, then fix.

Spatter effect. Arrange the masking shapes and spread the colour by rubbing the brush over the metal grille.

Alter the position of the masks, then apply a second colour.

Adding paste to paint

This technique is a very old one and produces extremely novel effects, although these are often less spectacular than those already discussed. It also requires a certain amount of creative originality on the painter's part.

The beauty of this technique is that it allows for a considerable working time in which to develop a design, since the paste medium dries slowly and can be worked into, or over, while it is still wet.

An original composition, showing the use of paint with added paste. F. Capart.

Equipment and materials

You require a smooth working surface, something like marble, glass or formica, and this should be larger than your sheet of paper.

You will also need a selection of round or flat brushes, paint jars, spatulas, scrapers, and a rubber or plastic comb suitable for obtaining wood-grain effects. Plus, a saucepan and a wooden spoon to prepare the paste and some liquid glycerine and soap.

Paper

This must be resistant, non-absorbent, and relatively smooth.

Colours

All soluble media will be suitable, such as Chinese ink, soluble ink, and acrylic and gouache paints. These are then mixed with suitable pastes, either a starch or flour-based paste.

Paste preparation

Starch paste

Whatever quantity is required, the proportion should remain the same; one measure of starch to nine of water. One jar of starch to nine of water will cover about fifteen sheets of paper.

To prepare the paste pour the starch into a saucepan, work in one measure of water, then add the remainder, mixing thoroughly to avoid any lumps. Heat to boiling-point, mixing continuously with a wooden spoon. When the liquid begins to simmer, remove it from the heat and add a dessertspoonful of diluted glycerine and liquid soap. Mix in well and leave to cool for about fifteen minutes, stirring occasionally. The soap and glycerine provide a smooth finish and also fix the pigments.

Flour paste

Prepare in the same way as given for starch paste, but adjust the measure to one part of flour to five parts of water.

Preparation of colours

Tube or powdered colours should first be diluted with water, while remaining fairly concentrated. Liquid colours may be used just as they come.

Add to each jar of paint enough cold paste to fill it. About one-quarter paint to three-quarters paste is an ideal mix but this must be modified to suit the intensity required. With your brush, try out the colours on a separate piece of paper and correct the proportion, if necessary, to obtain the required tonal depth.

Materials and equipment for painting with added paste. Paper Sample, Florent Rousseau.

Opposite: **Wave effect obtained with a brush.** Stéphane Ipert.

Brushing in the coloured paste.

Application

Load a brush with coloured paste and cover the whole surface with a regular stroke. The glazed working surface beneath the paper can be used to take any surplus paste, if this is brushed beyond the paper's edge.

The starch should not be too thick, as the raised surface will make any additional decorating more difficult. On the other hand, if it is too thin, it will dry too quickly to allow continuous decoration.

If required, add a final coat of paste to ensure a smooth surface.

Painting with several colours

This technique is the same as for adding paste to paint, but each colour requires its own specific brush. Diverse applications are possible, whether worked in or to give a completely random effect.

Arrange your tints either in bands, overlapping to obtain a gradated effect, or as a 'mosaic'. Before embarking on any superimposition of designs, check that the paste surface is smooth.

If it is not, use a brush to eliminate any roughness, but work quickly so that the solution does not have time to dry out.

Try an experiment by drawing with your fingers. Pass your index finger over the paste and notice the patina this produces. This simple action will tell you a lot about the medium's possibilities. Draw freely, as any careless stroke can be removed by restoring the original smoothness.

For another exercise, take a clean brush and apply it to the paste surface in an evenly spaced, circular movement. A wave effect should thus be created.

Variations

There are many and varied possibilities with this technique because of the great diversity of tools available for the task. Spatulas, forks, scrapers, large-toothed combs, rollers and sponges will all produce different effects.

Remember to remove surplus paste from these instruments with a clean cloth after use.

Special types of paste decoration

Example of a scraper design. Stéphane Ipert.

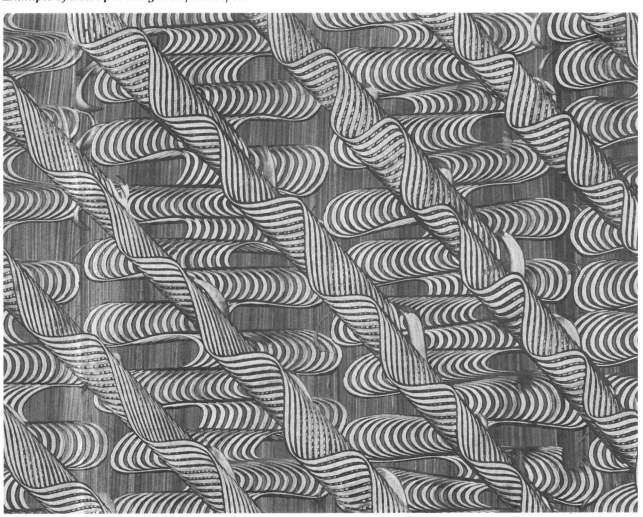

Using spatulas and scrapers

Take a spatula and apply the paint with added paste in a spiral, sideways motion to create a 'ribbon' effect. Alternatively, attempt a criss-cross effect over the whole surface, to give a sense of perspective. The same effects can be achieved with a scraper.

Imitation wood graining

For this effect use a special rubber or plastic comb, which can be obtained to reproduce wood graining. A metal comb may scratch the paper.

After pasting over the sheet, apply the comb from top to bottom with a spiralling movement, made lightly and evenly. This will suggest the knots in timber. Place your bands side by side without overlapping.

Printing effects

These are virtually limitless but try experimenting with the following two suggestions.

Having laid on a smooth paint with added paste surface, use some object, such as a piece of mesh, rumpled paper or a fragment of glass, which will leave a characteristic print. Alternatively, apply the paste to a similar object, then use this to print out a pattern on to your sheet of paper.

Composition using a spatula. Florent Rousseau.

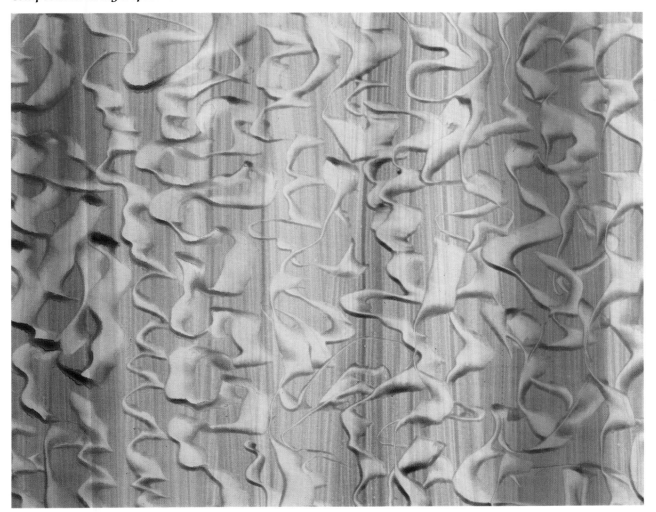

Separated papers

For this technique, paint with flour-paste added is the best medium, as it has a firmer consistency.

Apply coloured paste to your first sheet of paper in regular layers, both lengthwise and laterally. Take a sheet of identical paper, and repeat this process, then place one on top of the other, pasted sides together. Rub the back of the paper with the palm of your hand, then slowly separate the sheets.

A characteristic 'network' effect will result, resembling leaves or feathers. Clarity of design depends upon the consistency and the fluidity of the medium used.

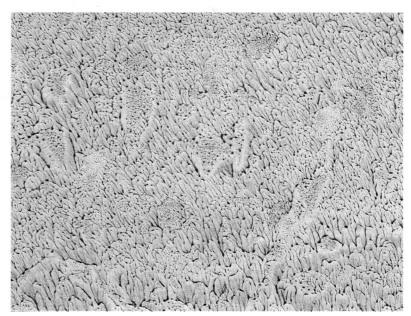

Example of a single-tone separated paper.
Stéphane Ipert.

Separating papers; pull the two sheets apart evenly.

Opposite: **Print of a grille loaded with coloured paste and the application of wood fragments.**

Drying the papers

Lay out the sheets of paper flat on a newspaper. The length of drying time depends upon the thickness of the paste and, on average, three or four hours are enough, but it is wise to allow a complete day. Once they are thoroughly dry, plac the sheets beneath weights to flatten them completely.

Figurative design over a two-colour background. U. Sovetti.

Masking techniques

These apply to all forms of decoration involving the use of masking fluids, such as gutta in the painting of silk. With this method you can obtain subtle and fantastic effects.

Pastel design obtained with masks and pigments. *Florent Rousseau.*

Equipment and materials

Use the same type of paper for this technique as recommended for the impressionist effects, see page 35. Avoid very absorbent papers.

Among several kinds of masking fluids obtainable, gum arabic and synthetic gums are recommended.

Masking fluids

Gum arabic can be bought either dissolved or in granular form. This medium penetrates the paper.

Synthetic gums are ready for use, either as a suitable drawing medium, or for relief composition. Their latex base causes rapid drying and creates a protective paint-repellent surface, which does not require a fixative.

Colours

Preferably use oil-based printing inks diluted with white spirit, which will allow the colours to be absorbed by the paper.

Before beginning, assemble a number of different-sized brushes, paint jars, a sponge and some spatulas.

Preparing and applying the masking fluid

When using a ready-made product, such as gum arabic or drawing gum, no special preparation is needed, but synthetic gum must be stirred before use and gum arabic further dissolved. Gum arabic crystals must first be converted to a thick paste, then a little more water added.

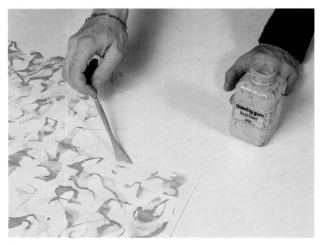

Using a spatula to apply drawing gum as a masking agent.

Whatever the product to be used, the method of application does not vary. The fluid can be applied directly to the paper with a brush or a spatula. Indirect treatments, however, will produce diffused effects. Try spreading the masking fluid on to a sheet of glass, then apply your paper on top of this.

Results will differ according to the medium used. Gum arabic with its penetrative quality will produce more subtle effects, whereas synthetic gum gives a more defined composition.

In all cases, leave the masking fluid to dry for twenty minutes before applying the colours.

Preparing and applying the colours

Dilute solid oil-based printing ink with white spirit to the following measures; one walnut-sized measure of ink to ten dessertspoonfuls of solvent. Prepare at least one jar of colour. This should not be too dark, but tend towards a pale shade of the colour, which is better suited to these effects.

Example using gum arabic as a masking fluid. The fluid was applied with a brush and a double layer of colour added.
Florent Rousseau.

Beside your working surface, place the jars of colour and brushes. Dip the brush into the first colour of your choice, then spread it in straight lines over the paper, ignoring the masked areas. Once the sheet is completely covered, leave it to dry flat.

At first, keep to a single colour, but as you progress in expertise, you can experiment with two or three colours.

Removing masking fluid

This should be done by gently stroking the gum with a finger, or a cloth, in the case of latex gum. For gum arabic, however, use a damp sponge. Avoid rumpling or creasing the paper when you apply this, and rinse the sponge from time to time.

The removal of the masking gum reveals, once again, the background tinting of the original paper. At least two applications of this procedure will be needed to provide an interesting design.

Painting with the first colour.

Rubbing away the masking gum with a cloth.

Painting with a second colour, after a new application of gum.

30

Using stencils

Stencils may be used to mask out either regular or random areas of colour.

Stencils

These offer enormous variety of shape and pictorial effect and many different devices may be employed. *Natural stencils* Feathers, leaves, grasses, pebbles and wood bark. *Artificial stencils* Transparent plastic, cut card, metal meshes and wooden shapes.

Colours

Acrylic aerosol paints are recommended as these give better coverage and allow for a more careful finish, but please follow the maker's instructions. An airbrush can also be used to vapourize the colour, but it is best to do this outdoors.

Example showing the repetition of the masking and colouring process. *Florent Rousseau.*

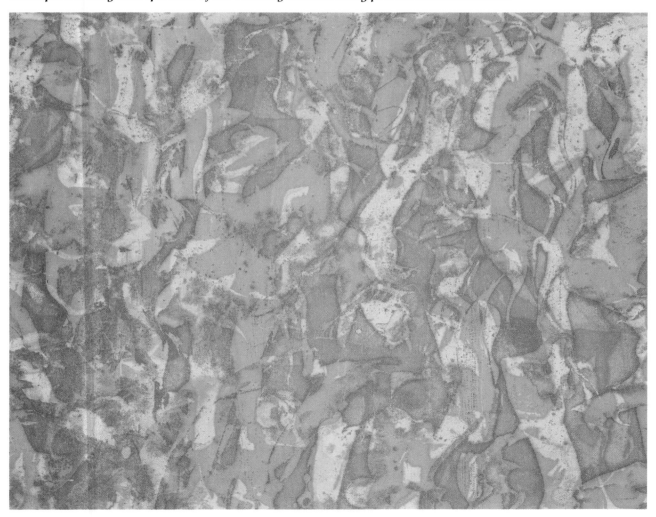

Placing the stencils

Aim for originality, either with a distributed or compact placement of the stencils. Rearrange them until you have obtained a pleasing artistic composition.

After allowing the first coat of paint to dry, you can continue to rearrange the stencils, then apply another layer of contrasting colour. In this way you can continue to build up layers of colour and pattern to achieve striking effects of perspective.

Example showing the stencils in position, then irregular spraying with an aerosol over the entire sheet.

Perspective effect. *Florent Rousseau.*

32

Batik decorated papers

This process may be applied both to paper and to fabrics, and its basic concept is similar to that of the stencil or masking techniques. There are several variations of batik, among them folded batik, and batik using wax. These normally relate to fabric, although these methods were used on 'Java' paper at the beginning of this century. Folding, in particular, gives very original and variegated effects.

Folded batik

The paper is first folded, then tinted with different colours. Once unfolded again, it reveals a multicoloured mosaic pattern which is uniformly spread over the paper, like marquetry. The hues melt gently into each other and gather along the crease lines.

Paper

This should be thin and permeable, somewhere between 15 and 30gm (½ and 1oz) to the square metre (yard). Japanese silk paper fulfils these conditions and is well suited to the batik technique.

Colours

Water-soluble pigments suitable for textiles, such as soluble or Chinese inks, are recommended. They are used either pure or diluted, according to your requirements.

Equipment

Cloths for removing surplus colours and various glass jars to contain the colours.

Folding the paper

This preliminary stage will determine your whole design and there are two basic methods; fan-shaped folds and rectangular folds. The former produce designs which converge on a single point, such as circles and spirals, and the latter form parallel lines and right-angled geometric shapes.

For a fan-shaped design take a piece of paper about 21 × 29cm (8½ × 11½in) and fold it into four. Where all four corners meet at the centre point, begin folding the paper back on itself across the long edge, to form fan-shaped pleats. For a rectangular format, fold the paper back on itself across the whole width to form accordion pleats, see diagrams. In both instances, the more often you fold the paper the more intricate the design you will achieve.

Tinting

Begin by dipping each corner of your folded sheet of paper into one colour, and this will gradually permeate the paper. Do this rapidly in

Rectangular folds

a) **Fold the paper into an accordion-pleated strip.**

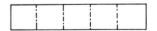

b) **Pleat the strip from left to right through all the layers.**

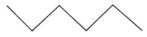

c) **The final fold.**

Remember to keep tightly folded when colouring.

Apply a different tint to each corner of the folded sheet.

order to avoid overloading. Remove from the colour and wipe off surplus with a cloth. Repeat as many times as you like, using other colours on the corners or edges of the folds. You may also wish to leave parts untouched by colour.

Now unfold the paper gently and leave to dry flat, for about half an hour. If the paper is too fragile, however, it is wiser to unfold it after it is dry.

Precaution

These papers are extremely fragile, especially when soaked in paint. Once dry, they should be ironed at a heat suitable for silk, but make sure you put a sheet of white paper over the batik to avoid staining. Once ironed, fix the paint lightly with a suitable aerosol fixative. It is sometimes necessary to apply a backing sheet of plain paper as a strengthener before using your painted paper.

Folded batik using four colours. *Stéphane Ipert.*

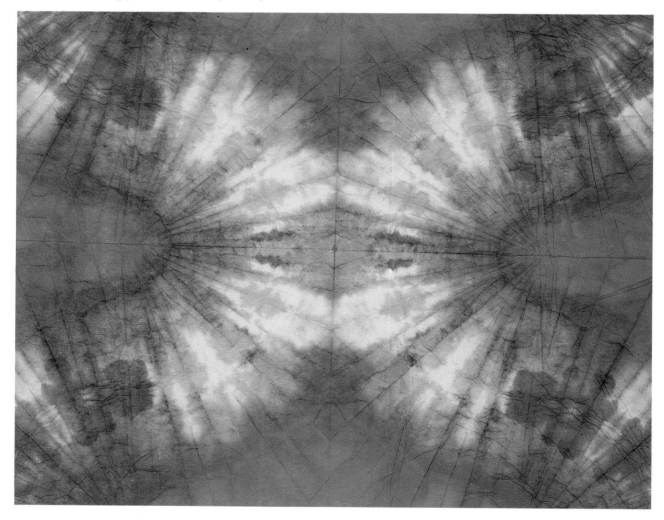

Making impressions

These techniques are relatively simple to execute and provide a remarkable variety of decoration. As they are similar to the methods used to produce linocuts, some of them enable several duplicate sheets to be made.

The choice of paper you intend to use is very important, as this will determine the clarity of the printing. Although all types of paper will take an impression, the best results will be obtained from non-absorbent paper, with a slightly shiny surface. Good quality paper used in the printing trade is an excellent medium.

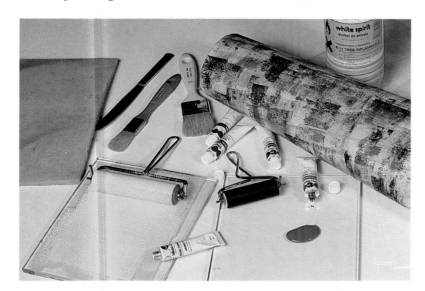

Equipment and materials

Colours

Oil-based printing ink in tubes should be used. These have 'body', can be intermixed, and are soluble in white spirit, which also serves to clean your tools.

Inking-palette

You will need a sheet of glass about 30 × 30cm (12 × 12in). In fact, it is worth having several such sheets in order to save the constant cleaning of one during work.

Rollers

These are printing rollers made of rubber. They can be bought in art shops or in DIY stores. You should have several of different sizes, so as to obtain a variety of designs.

Certain techniques also call for gouges in order to sculpt the roller. Indeed, almost any object which has a relief surface can create a print. House and garden provide an endless supply of usable artefacts that may suggest novel motifs, such as bobbins, potatoes and leaves.

Preparation of colours

Oil-based printing ink requires no previous preparation. Place your tubes of colour, as well as the sheet of glass, at the right of your working surface. The roller may be inked either wholly or in part.

Using a fully inked roller

This method produces a design of vertical, horizontal and diagonal lines, giving textural and perspective effects.

The amount of ink used depends upon the extent of the design. Squeeze sufficient ink from a tube on to the centre of your sheet of glass. Then push your roller in all directions, from top to bottom and

Composition demonstrating several techniques, including direct printing and impressions with a sculpted roller. Florent Rousseau.

side to side of the glass, until both roller and glass are well covered. To make sure the colours are well blended, the inks should first be mixed with a knife on the edge of the sheet of glass and then spread by using the roller. Direct mixing with the roller produces unsatisfactory results.

Varied techniques with the roller

Once the roller is inked, your first attempt should consist of rolling it in a continuous movement over the paper surface. Grasp the roller with your whole hand, then apply it after lining it up with the bottom of the sheet, regulating your speed and pressure. Too great a pressure will cause irregular spreading of the ink.

Once the first colour is dry, you may prepare a second colour, or even three or more. Clean both the roller and the glass with white spirit, apply the new ink and load the roller. This new colour can either juxtapose the previous one or can be lightly applied over it. Cover the whole sheet of paper.

Mosaic effects

These are produced by a variation in roller technique. Instead of continuous rolling, you may interrupt the process and reapply the roller at a new point, retaining or changing its direction, according to the effect required. By varying the colour as well as the direction, you achieve a geometrical pattern, giving a relief effect by superimposition.

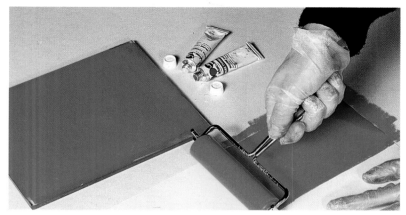

The roller is fully inked, then applied to the paper.

The roller is fully inked, then applied in square and rectangular blocks.

A fresh colour is overlayed.

Partial inking of the roller

This method will produce lovely effects, similar to algae and feathers, with the appearance of a thick impasto style of painting.

Place your chosen inks side by side on the sheet of glass without mixing them, then pass the roller over them from top to bottom without exerting too much pressure.

Lay the roller gently on the paper and roll it, equally gently, so that the colours stick well to the surface, producing a network effect resembling algae. One application will be sufficient for a good impression in relief. Renew the ink on the roller with the same colours and the same amount of pigment in order to achieve identical effects over the whole sheet of paper.

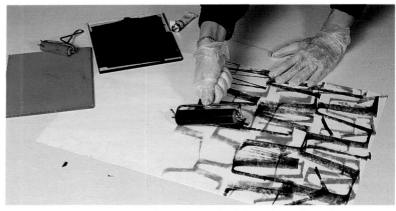

The roller is fully inked, then applied with a pivotal motion.

'Ribbon' effect on a ground of gradated soluble ink.
Florent Rousseau.

'Ribbon' effect.

Composition on a gradated background in soluble ink, using partial inking of the roller.
Florent Rousseau.

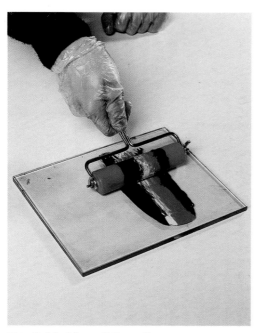

*Partial inking of the roller
with four colours.*

*Having inked the roller thickly, apply it to the sheet of paper
but not too heavily.*

Opposite: **Composition obtained with
partial inking of the roller.**
Florent Rousseau.

41

Thread effects

Prepare two rollers before you begin, an ordinary one to ink over the sheet of glass, and another to produce a wiry impression. To obtain this effect, wrap thin string round and round the rubber of the roller and glue the ends together.

Once the roller is completely inked in one hue, make sure that the ink is well spread over the thread. Apply the roller to the paper as previously instructed. The resultant effect combines well with other motifs, and it can be used over any coloured background, whether plain or variegated.

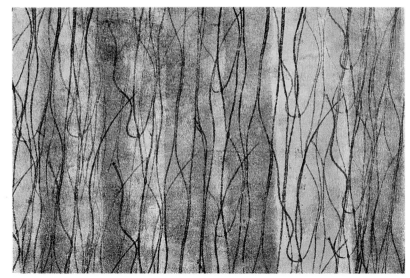

Thread impression on a previously inked background.
Florent Rousseau.

Using a sculpted roller

This method creates a novel printing effect which can be repeated indefinitely. Buy linocutting tools, in particular gouges which can be used to carve into the rubber of the roller. The ink will only cover the surface area which remains raised.

You will need to spend quite a lot of time and be absolutely precise in your movements for this type of decoration, but originality of effect justifies the effort! The inking and application of the roller are the same as previously described.

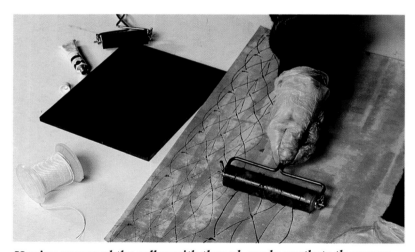

Having wrapped the roller with thread, apply gently to the paper.

Spot impressions

To achieve this effect, pour a few drops of white spirit on to the glass, having already inked it, then pass the roller over it. The spirit will dilute the ink perceptibly and the print will show a sequence of more or less regular spots well spread out.

42

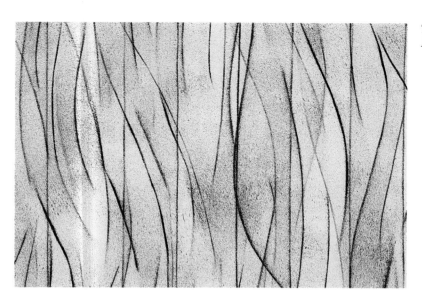

Thread printing on spattered paper.
Florent Rousseau.

Detail from a composition using a sculpted roller. *Florent Rousseau.*

Pour some drops of white spirit on to the inked sheet of glass, then pass the roller over it. The oil-based printing ink will be lightly diluted during application.

Example of 'spot' printing with several colours. *Florent Rousseau.*

Direct printing techniques

Beautiful and interestingly shaped objects make very decorative printing motifs. Some, such as the leaves of trees with their indented outlines, require no special preparation. Others, despite what may appear to be a lack of aesthetic charm, may nevertheless contribute to your design.

The effect is achieved by the grouping and repetition of the decorative elements. Their distribution can be left to chance, or can adhere to some geometrical arrangement. An exhaustive list of usable objects is not given here, because personal selection is the best rule to follow and every artist must search for his or her own ideas and techniques. Among other materials, however, plastic and wooden objects provide excellent designs.

Begin by inking over the whole surface of the sheet of glass and place the objects to be printed on to it, then apply them to the paper with a light pressure. To obtain a clear print, it is advisable to lay a piece of either felting or foam rubber under the sheet of paper.

Drying

Hang the finished sheet of paper on a line with clothes-pegs in an airy spot. The drying time can vary from two days to a week, depending on the quantity of ink used.

Example of direct printing achieved with a grille made of plastic, previously inked. Florent Rousseau.

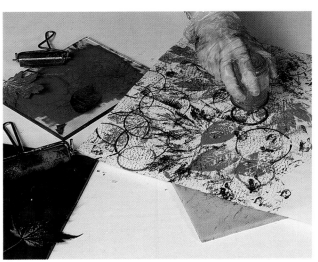

Direct printing. Various objects and plant forms have been used and thin foam rubber has been placed beneath the sheet of paper.

Using gloss-coated papers

Except for the type of paper used, this technique does not entail any special working method. It lends itself to modern decorative effects extremely well.

Gloss-coated papers are thick and their upper face is extremely smooth and shiny. Various weights and finishes may be purchased from an art shop, but you will need to experiment to find which gives you the results you require. They work best with direct treatment methods, such as making impressions and the enterprising employment of stencils, or masking gum.

Equipment and materials

Paper

Hot-pressed with a glossy surface.

Colours

Pigments should be soluble in solvents, such as lighter fuel, or pure alcohol obtained from a chemist. You can use certain dyes or stains for this purpose, but their preparation is rather difficult. A beginner should opt for pure alcohol, which is less effective but easier to handle! Some colours, such as those achieved with marker pens, are not resistant to light and will gradually disappear.

Solvents

Solvents such as acetone, alcohol and methylated spirits, produce special effects, but they must be kept in sealed glass containers because they are poisonous or inflammable, so beware of their escaping vapours! It is wise to work in a well-aired room and to wear plastic gloves and under no circumstance smoke when using them.

Masking areas

Use a tube of gum or glue with which you can draw as your masking agent.

Colours should be applied with a brush, or pieces of felt rolled on to the end of a wooden stick.

Masked composition. Stéphane Ipert.

Other equipment

A large sheet of glass on which to work, considerably larger than your sheet of paper.

Colour preparation and application

Dilute your powder pigments with a suitable vehicle, such as alcohol, according to the measure suggested by the manufacturer. Always try out the colour density and penetration on a scrap of paper first.

For plain backgrounds, spread the colour with a piece of felt soaked in paint, or with a brush. It should permeate the paper's thickness through the glossy surface and it may even spread of its own accord, up to a point. The result is usually a pastel and brilliant effect.

By adding certain solvents such as acetone to the pigments, mother-of-pearl and iridescent effects can be attained. Other media will enable you to thin the colours already applied. Don't superimpose more than three colours, however, for fear of a grey or muddy result.

Masking effects

Apply the masking agent to an untouched, or previously painted sheet of paper with either a brush or spatula. Leave to dry, then apply the colour and allow this to dry. Rub away the mask, whether totally or partially, then apply the fresh colour. To complete, remove any remaining masking agent.